NEWS FROM NEW CYTHERA

A Report of Bougainville's Voyage, 1766–1769

A PUBLICATION FROM THE JAMES FORD BELL LIBRARY
AT THE UNIVERSITY OF MINNESOTA

News from New Cythera

A REPORT OF BOUGAINVILLE'S VOYAGE
1766–1769

EDITED BY L. DAVIS HAMMOND

The University of Minnesota Press, Minneapolis

F THE three issues of the *Newsletter* that were apparently published, the undated issue from the James Ford Bell Library is the basis of this first English edition. It is not possible to determine whether or not the undated issue was published before or after the other two issues, which were dated July 20, 1769, and August 1, 1769. This first published account of Bougainville's voyage probably had a sizable printing and enjoyed a wide sale, but only a very few copies have survived.

The full title, *Relation de la découverte que vient de faire Mr. de Bouguainville* [sic], *d'une Isle qu'il a nommée La Nouvelle Cythere*, reveals the emphasis that was placed on the discovery of an island which Bougainville had named New Cythera, now Tahiti. In choosing the name New Cythera, Bougainville paid tribute to the pleasures that had been found on Tahiti. At the island of Cythera, now known as Cerigo, the Greek goddess of love and beauty, Aphrodite, supposedly first rose out of the sea.

About two years after the *Newsletter*, Bougainville published his official account of the voyage, *Voyage autour du monde, par la frégate du Roi La Boudeuse, et la flûte l'Étoile*. Here, the Tahiti visit was placed in a more subdued light, but to the Frenchmen who rèad the *Relation* of 1769 Tahiti represented a paradise of natural life far from the complexities of European civilization.

Professor Hammond has supplied notes to his translation of the *Newsletter*, together with an introduction that places it in a historical setting and a commentary that describes its impact on Bougainville's countrymen. The translations from other French sources are also Professor Hammond's. In making this rare leaflet available, the James Ford Bell Library is following its tradition of sharing its resources with the public.

John Parker, CURATOR

JAMES FORD BELL LIBRARY

March, 1970

Introduction

N JULY 1769, a leaflet telling of Louis Antoine de Bougainville's great voyage around the world and of his sensational "discovery" appeared in France. The discovery was the island Tahiti, to which Bougainville gave the alluring epithet of New Cythera. Here at last was a prestigious achievement for the French in an age when such accomplishments seemed to have become the exclusive privilege of the English.

In addition to appealing to the nationalistic sentiments of the French, this news also stimulated the popular imagination, much the way news of the moon shots would do two hundred years later. Each century has had its particular obsession: the main concern during the sixteenth century was with the discovery of new continents; during the eighteenth century men were fascinated with islands (an obvious example is the representative hero, Robinson Crusoe), and Bougainville's discovery of Tahiti was sufficient to make him a public figure, although his voyage had other more important scientific and political implications.

Bougainville's voyage should be seen against the background of the Seven Years War, which dominates the history of the mid-eighteenth century. This was a war, mainly for empire, waged between France and England on land and sea. Although not declared until 1756 it began in 1754 with a series of French military successes, and ended in 1763 with the signing of the Treaty of Paris, which signified the near collapse of the French empire and conversely the beginning of England's reign as the greatest world power. The terms of peace secured for England Canada, Senegal, St. Vincent, Tobago, and the Grenadines, in addition to Minorca's return. England also gained Florida from Spain; while France had to give Spain Louisiana. In India France was allowed to keep only the factories which she had established before 1749. England was not without mercy, for she returned several spoils of war: Manila and Havana were given back to Spain, and Martinique, St. Lucia, Gorée, and the St. Lawrence and Newfoundland fisheries, including St. Pierre and Miquelon, were returned to France. The peace seemed scandalous to the English prime minister, William Pitt, but wonderfully generous to the Duc de Choiseul, who, at that time, was the French minister of war and marine. And yet France's vast overseas empire was largely disintegrated: she still possessed St. Dominique, Ile de France (now Mauritius), Bourbon (now Réunion

4

Island), and some trading posts on Sumatra, but even these paltry remnants of her previous grandeur were at the mercy of her powerful enemies. This state of affairs was in many ways the result of French naval weakness. Her lack of seamen, of fighting ships, and of adequate logistical support for extended maritime war explains in large measure the disaster France suffered as an imperial power.

Nevertheless, a little more than a decade after this defeat France had her revenge. By 1778 the American colonies had successfully resisted England, and it was England's turn to seek peace. William Pitt, the man who had been most responsible for the humiliation of France during the nine years of war on the Continent and especially on the sea, spoke on April 7, 1778, against a motion to negotiate with the Americans and their ally, France: "Shall a people that fifteen years ago was the terror of the world," he asked the House of Lords, "now stoop so low as to tell its ancient inveterate foe: 'Take all we have, only give us peace?' "[1] The outraged Englishman's question eloquently bears witness to an accomplished fact: the astonishing rebirth of France as a world power. Bougainville's circumnavigation in 1766–69 secured for him a high place among the world's sailors and geographers; but more than that it brought considerable prestige to his country and was an episode in the dramatic recovery of power to which Pitt alluded.

But all this is projection and to gain some understanding of why and how Bougainville's voyage around the world came about, it would be helpful to look back briefly at the man's life. Bougainville was born into a family of the grande bourgeoisie on November 12, 1729, in Paris. His father, Pierre-Yves de Bougainville, was a lawyer. His mother was Marie-Françoise d'Arboulin de Bougainville. In 1741 his father was given a title of nobility, which opened up new career possibilities for the young Bougainville. He had an excellent classical education and showed a remarkable talent for mathematics. The attraction of a scholarly life was strengthened by the influence of his older brother, Jean-Pierre, who had assumed the responsibility for his brother's education and was himself fascinated with geography and the sciences related to it. But at the same time Bougainville wanted a nobleman's career in the military. He boldly combined these two ambitions. In the early 1750's he joined the Mousquetaires Noirs, a service which gave him distinction and access to the court. Early in 1754 Bougainville was named aide-de-camp to General François de Chevert, the leading military strategist in France. His academic development was continued through study under two well-known mathematicians, Jean d'Alembert and Alexis Clairaut. The first part of his mathematical treatise, *Traité de calcul intégral,* was published when Bougainville was only 22, in 1751; the second part was published in 1755. On January 8, 1756, he was elected to membership in the Royal Society of London.

6

In October of 1754 Bougainville was made secretary
to the French embassy in London. This particular time of
his life seems to be a most important one. Indeed, given
the benefits of hindsight, it is tempting to see in this ex-
perience one of the principal sources for the future direction of Bougainville's career. While in London, Bougainville had an unequaled opportunity to learn at first
hand the intentions of his country's great rival to con-
solidate her naval and military supremacy. The English
First Lord of the Admiralty at the time was George Anson, who had commanded a squadron in the Pacific, ter-
rorized Spanish shipping, circumnavigated the world in
1740–44, and defeated the French off Finisterre in 1747.
Lord Anson's insistence that England's place in the world
depended significantly on her ability to control the South
Seas commercially and militarily did not escape Bougainville's attention. And he could not have failed to realize
that France's power and stature would be determined by
her naval capacity and by the extension of her colonies.
But any expeditions into the Pacific by France were ham-
pered by her lack of suitable bases: Spain controlled the
Straits of Magellan and Cape Horn; Spain and Portugal
had in their power all ports in South America. The alter-
native was to send ships via the Cape of Good Hope to
Ile de France and then eastward. The French settlements
in India were not of real value in such a voyage; France
needed bases in the Far East and Bougainville no doubt
wished that the fashionable literary society which was so

influential in his own country would look beyond the borders of Europe, as the English had done.

Two years after this important stay in London Bougainville became actively involved in the political struggle between France and England. As an aide-de-camp of the Marquis de Montcalm, commander of the French troops in Canada, Bougainville left with him for the New World in March 1756. He fought in several French victories, including one in which he was slightly wounded. Bougainville was sent home to present the needs of the governor, the Marquis de Vaudreuil, and of Montcalm to the French court. His request for more reinforcements and money is reputed to have been denied by Nicolas Renée Berryer, minister of pleas, who explained that when there is a fire in the house, one does not bother about the stables — to which Bougainville replied that at least Berryer would not be accused of speaking "horse sense."[2] The anecdote may be apocryphal; in any event it is instructive about French priorities (and about Bougainville's urbanity). Bougainville thus was made acutely aware of his country's lack of serious commitment to its overseas territories, its financial inability to sustain them, and the weakness which inevitably resulted from this. With the few troops he was given, Bougainville returned to Canada and rejoined the army east of Quebec. On September 13, 1759, the French lost the decisive battle of the Plains of Abraham and Quebec was occupied soon afterwards. Bougainville remained with the retreating French army and was present at its defeat in September of the next year at Montreal. Governor de Vaudreuil then signed Canada over to the English and Bougainville sailed for France as a prisoner of war on parole.

The country to which Bougainville returned was tired of a war which dragged on in Europe though the outcome was no longer in question. Nor was there any doubt on the part of many Frenchmen that when the peace came it would be temporary. Bougainville believed that a key to the regaining of French power could be found in colonial enterprises. In the "Preliminary Discourse" which he later wrote to preface his account of his circumnavigation Bougainville exhorts his country to amend its ways and to awake to the potentials which he sensed and was eager to exploit. Although the Treaty of Paris is not specifically mentioned, it helps explain the nationalistic tone of the "Discourse." But even before the war ended and the treaty was signed, Bougainville began to make his plans.

Bougainville wanted to fit out an expedition and settle a colony. He had several influential relatives who shared his views on colonial enterprises and could be of assistance. Foremost among these was his uncle, Jean-Potentien d'Arboulin, a man of many talents who had the confidence of the king's mistress, Madame de Pompadour, and immense personal wealth. As already noted, Bougainville's brother was a member of the literary circles interested in geography and could aid his brother with invaluable contacts. A cousin, Bougainville de Nerville, was an advocate of French colonies and later played a major role in Bougainville's colony. But the biggest impetus to Bougainville's plans came from outside his family, in the person of Duc Etienne François de Choiseul, the minister of foreign affairs. Choiseul knew that France would have to rebuild her strength for another struggle with England. And like Bougainville, Choiseul believed that establishing colonies was important in such rebuilding. Choiseul employed Bougainville in his service on a number of diplomatic missions and was instrumental in getting the king's permission for Bougainville to carry out his project.

Where should a French colony be located? Bougainville's choice for a site was the Malouine Islands (now known as the Falkland Islands, the name the English had given them), off the coast of Argentina. They were uninhabited and seemingly unclaimed. Bougainville believed that it would be a good place to establish a settlement for some unhappy Acadians displaced by the surrender of the French in Canada. He was interested in gaining a lucrative monopoly for himself and at the same time he hoped to secure for France what he thought would become a rich commercial outpost. He also was certain that such an undertaking would result inevitably in the enrichment of the natural sciences, and especially in the advancement of geography. Most important, a col-

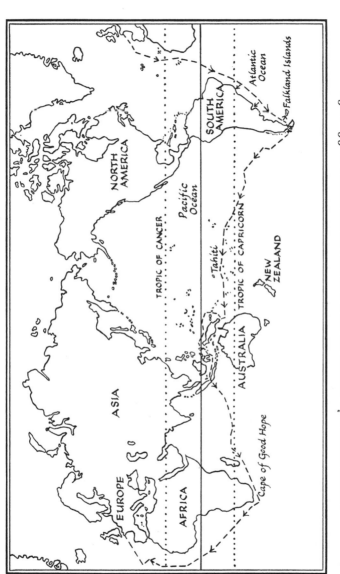

BOUGAINVILLE'S ROUTE IN THE CIRCUMNAVIGATION 1766–1769

ony located in the Malouines would have strategic advantages for France in both defense and offense.

Bougainville recalled Lord Anson's account of his own
voyage around the world:

Since as our fleets are at present superior to those of the whole
world united, it must be a matchless degree of supineness or
mean-spiritedness, if we permitted any of the advantages which
new discoveries or a more extended navigation may produce to
mankind, to be ravished from us.

As therefore it appears that all our future expeditions to the
South Seas must run a considerable risque of proving abortive,
whilst we are under the necessity of touching at *Brazil* in our
passage thither, an expedient that might relieve us from this
difficulty, would surely be a subject worthy of the attention of
the Public; and this seems capable of being effected, by the
discovery of some place more to the southward, where ships
might refresh and supply themselves with the necessary sea-
stock for their voyage round Cape *Horn*. And we have in reality
the imperfect knowledge of two places, which might perhaps,
on examination, prove extremely convenient for this purpose;
the first of them is *Pepys's* Island, in the latitude of 47°
South . . . the second is Falkland's Isles, in the latitude of
51 and 1/2 degrees nearly South of Pepys's Island . . . This
[a post in one of these two places], even in a time of peace,
might be of great consequence to this Nation; and, in a time of
war, would make us masters of those seas.[3]

Bougainville explicitly put forward, in terms which
are closely parallel to these words, the political consid-
erations which motivated his expedition. He believed that
it was a question of competing with the English at their
own strategy of domination:

England, mistress of Canada by the terms of the peace treaty, and mistress of the sea because of a navy incomparably superior to those of all the rest of Europe together, seemed to me to lack only posts in the South Seas.

By securing the sources of wealth through such posts, England was carrying out the dream of universal monarchy falsely imputed to Louis XIV. Anson had advised his nation to establish herself on the Malouine Islands, whose position is the key to the South Seas. What better thing could England do in the interlude of such a peace than to lay hold of an outpost which would make her the ruler of Europe should war break out? I thought that France should prevent the English from doing this, and I got permission to explore these islands and to create there a settlement, at my own expense, together with my cousin de Nerville and my uncle d'Arboulin, which would secure the possession of the islands to France.[4]

This expedition to the Malouine Islands was proposed in 1761 and was actually begun in 1763. The French government approved of Bougainville's plan for a colony but had no funds to contribute. Hence, as proposed, the financing was shared by Bougainville, his cousin Bougainville de Nerville, and his uncle d'Arboulin. The landing was made at the Malouines on January 31, 1764. In April of that year Bougainville returned to France, leaving the colony under the leadership of de Nerville. Upon his return there in January of 1765 Bougainville found that the settlement was prospering and had every reason to believe that it would be successful.

A French colony on the Malouine Islands was not included in England's plans for that part of the world. The threat was obvious, and when John Byron was sent on his voyage of exploration in 1764 his instructions from his government included an order to visit the Malouines. When England learned from Byron that the French did indeed have a colony there, she laid plans for a colony of her own on these islands. If France could claim the Malouines, England could also — by right of prior discovery. But by now, Spain was involved as well, insisting that the Malouines were actually by geography a part of her holdings in South America and everybody else should stay away.

Rather than allow the English to settle the Malouines France decided to honor the Spanish claim. And so Bougainville was told to dissolve his colony. To soften the disappointment, the king offered Bougainville the governorship of Ile de France and Bourbon. This did not appeal to Bougainville, who asked instead to be allowed to make a voyage around the world. The Spanish king had offered to pay the expenses that Bougainville had incurred in establishing the colony, and the first order of business Bougainville was to complete on his voyage was to officially hand over to France's ally, Spain, the French settlement on the Malouine Islands.

But if the transferal of this colony in its infancy to Spain was the immediate and official objective of Bougainville's expedition of 1766–69, an obvious if unstated expectation was that Bougainville would seek new colonial outposts in the Pacific to replace those lost in the recent war. Settlements near the Philippines were of particular interest, since trade with China was going to have to make up for the newly cut-off trade with India. In fact, Bougainville had explicit instructions to keep a lookout for islands off the Chinese coast which could serve as warehouses for the Compagnie des Indes in its trade with China. A further purpose of the voyage was to bring to the important French colony on Ile de France certain plants and spices whose cultivation would enrich the island's economy and, not incidentally, advance Bougainville's own fortune.

But Bougainville's undertaking cannot be wholly understood as a nationalistic or a commercial adventure in expansionism, for a genuine scientific curiosity also shaped it. Bougainville was educated in a time when there was a strong interest in the broad subject of science. Long before Bougainville became a soldier and finally a sailor he had an orientation toward natural history. Some of the scientific questions current in his day could only be answered by a voyage such as Bougainville had planned. These questions were outlined by Pierre Louis Moreau de Maupertuis, one of the foremost scientific figures of Europe during this period.

In a discourse addressed to Frederick II of Prussia in 1752, entitled *Lettre sur le progrès des sciences*, Maupertuis set forth three areas of investigation which would be of general service to mankind, and which would especially benefit the progress of science. The first and most important of these was the search for the Terres Austra-les. As the realities of America proved increasingly at variance with the vision of an earthly paradise, hopes for fulfilling this vision were transferred to other regions less well known, and the Terres Australes became the focus of those who dreamed of a new world beyond the New World. The existence of such a place had been suggested by the great French naturalist Georges Leclerc, Comte de Buffon, in his *Théorie de la terre* in 1749, and Charles de Brosses perpetuated the notion in his *Histoire des Navigations aux Terres Australes* (1756); Maupertuis' claim that the search for these lands was most important was not, therefore, an eccentric one. The second question which Maupertuis listed among the most important had to do with the Patagonians. It had been reported by eminent men that the inhabitants of Tierra del Fuego were giants, and Commodore Byron had confirmed this gigantism during his voyage of 1764–66. The Royal Society had taken up the argument, and there was considerable scientific clamor over it; once again, Maupertuis was simply representing the scientific community when he stated that investigation into this problem could lead to a significant advance of man's knowledge about the universe. The third item on Maupertuis' agenda was the discovery of a northern passage to Asia. He suggested that it probably was to be found via the North Pole. To this last project Bougainville addressed himself in his later years without ever being able to persuade his government to permit him to undertake the venture, but the first two can be considered as the scientific purposes of his celebrated voyage around the world in 1766–69.

Bougainville's investigation of the Patagonian giants and his search for the mysterious austral lands resulted in negative conclusions. The Patagonians were perhaps very broad in the shoulders, but they were not inordinately tall. The austral lands, he was quite sure, were an illusion, although he did not document this truth as Captain James Cook was to do so definitively in the course of his great voyages. But stating the scientific usefulness of Bougainville's voyage in terms of such negative discoveries as these should not obscure the fact that his exploit marked an essentially positive advance in man's attempt to know the true dimensions of his world. Carefully drawn maps are doubtless the most considerable end result of the expedition, and Bougainville's stature as a geographer, although it does not compare with that of his great contemporary Cook, is quite unassailable.

Bougainville wrote a fairly objective account of his trip in *Voyage autour du Monde*. However, this version of his voyage did not appear until two years after the publication of the *Newsletter* focusing on Bougainville's fortuitous discovery of Tahiti. The news about Tahiti and Aoutouru, the native of the island whom Bougainville had brought back with him, stimulated much popular excitement. This pleased the French government, for the excitement obscured the scientific and political aims

17

of Bougainville's voyage — which were likely to arouse suspicion in other nations. France was not the only country that tried to disguise the real motives behind circumnavigations. The British government had cleverly played up the issue of the Patagonian giants in order to divert curiosity from Byron's visit to the Malouine Islands during his expedition of 1764–66.

Translation

*T*HE POPULAR success of the *Newsletter* at the time is a reflection of the interest of Frenchmen in exploration and in any national accomplishment. The French public was weary of defeat — the country needed a taste of success and Bougainville had supplied it. However, because of the ephemeral nature of the publication, few copies have survived. For the first time this *Newsletter* appears in translation.

An Account of Mr. de Bougainville's recent discovery of an Island which he has named New Cythera

Mr. de Bougainville, commander of the king's frigate *La Boudeuse*, commissioned at Brest with 32 cannon and a crew of 230 men, and on which the Prince of Orange sailed as a passenger, left this harbor in October of 1766.[1] The king's storeship *L'Etoile* of Rochefort, with 20 cannon and 200 men, under Mr. de Giraudais, captain of a fire ship,[2] was also in Mr. de Bougainville's command.

On board these two ships, which have sailed around the world via the Straits of Magellan in the South Sea, were Mr. de Romainville, engineer, Mr. Camereau, physician and naturalist, and Mr. Veson, pilot and astronomer.[3]

The two ships set sail together from the roads of Rio de Janeiro for Montevideo, where they were to spend the winter and prepare for the passage through the Straits of Magellan, a passage which can only be undertaken between January and the end of April.[4]

The Straits of Magellan is a narrows, or channel, bounded on both sides by land and islands which are for the most part inhabited. Among others in the Straits, there is one island where the men are of gigantic size; the smallest of them are from eight to eight and a half feet tall;[5] they are white, and live like savages. The two ships of the king passed through the Button Straits and visited the Dutch East Indies, where diamonds and precious stones are mined; they sighted Sumatra and anchored at the island of Sastadia, a colony superior to the Ile de France.

Between the Straits of Magellan and Batavia, latitude ***** (it has not been possible to learn it, since Mr. de Bougainville, before leaving, ordered that no information on this subject be given out),[6] these two ships of the king discovered an ISLAND, unanimously named by the officers *New Cythera*. The climate of this island is mild and temperate, the air is pure and serene, and the sky there is very lovely. The island's inhabitants are very tall; the men are from six to six and a half feet tall, and the women are nearly the same size. These islanders are white, and their race is handsome. The women particularly are distinguished by the regularity of their features, their gentleness, and their natural affability. Both sexes have very beautiful teeth, and hair of different colors, like Europeans. The men let their beards grow; they wear a poncho or a sort of dalmatic of white bark which they weave and card themselves. They wear neither shoes nor pants, and go about bareheaded. The women are covered from the neck to the feet with a great veil made of very fine white bark. They are very hospitable, very gracious, and quick to caress. When they met one of the officers, or anyone else from the ships' crews, they went up to them and by song and demonstrative gesture expressed their joy; they would then take by the hand and envelop in their veil the European whom they had so wonderfully greeted. The husbands considered these signs of tenderness for their wives [that the Europeans then tendered] as a homage and an honor; these women are free of any base interest, and all their ambition is satisfied by a pendant or a cuff link which they attach to their ears. They are extremely loving to their children.

These islanders have a king whom they obey blindly; he has the power of life and death over them. They worship the sun as their first deity; there are two others besides, a god of good and a god of evil. They offer up to the god of good the first fruits of their agriculture, and to the spirit or god of evil they sacrifice human victims; women are not subjected to so cruel a law. Hurricanes, storms, and other public calamities are the sad signals of these barbarous sacrifices, carried out by order and will of the king. They choose the ugliest among them, someone who has a deformed limb, or who is not as white as the others, and dedicate him as a victim to the god of evil: they cover him with flowers, and a great throng of people accompanies him to the shore where he is cruelly killed by bleeding: the jugular vein is cut with a sort of knife of mother-of-pearl, or a sharp stone. The sacrificed victim is laid out on a wicker mat, dressed in all the ornaments which were his during his life; these are reddened with the victim's blood, and no islander would dare touch them or steal them for fear of exposing himself alone to the anger and vengeance of the god of evil.

These people have not yet known any commerce or trade; they have little canoes which are rather poorly constructed and badly joined together, for up until this discovery they had no idea of nails, caulking, and pitch. They use these canoes to do their fishing. In addition to their king, they have twelve chiefs. This king has no mark of distinction, unless it be that his cabin is a bit more spacious; and his sovereignty is hereditary. The soil of this vast country produces sugarcane naturally: but these people know neither how to use it, nor what it is. The land is fit for all the plants and produce of our islands of South America. The fruit which serves as their bread is the size of a melon, weighing from two to ten pounds; it is red inside, and tastes very good; they knead it with water and make of it a dough which is as nourishing a substance as bread, and which can be kept fresh for five or six months. On this island there are also plantains, much better than those from Saint Domingue and from Martinique: some of these are about as thick as a thigh. The islanders raise pigs, goats, and chickens, which are about the same there as in Europe; they eat their meat roasted over coals, or boiled;[7] their only drink is coconut milk, or water, which, according to the analysis made of it by the physician-naturalist, is much lighter than ours.

They eat and drink whenever hunger and thirst call, and have no set hours for their meals; they eat seated on mats of reed and drink from coconut shells. Their food, as has already been said, consists of grilled or boiled meat, and of fish which they catch with hooks of mother-of-pearl and with baskets or nets more or less like those of our fishermen; their food is served in dishes made of coconut shell.

On this island there are many very rare, very beautiful, and very curious birds, among which there is the *Lory*, whose plumage is variegated with the most beautiful and brilliant colors. There are parrots of every kind and of every color: one kind is the size of a wren with feathers of the loveliest royal blue and a very long tail.

The cockatoo, or *Pitacus-albus*, is a parrot, white like a swan, with a large black beak, and on the back as well as under the neck he has a tuft of feathers, like a reversed crest, of a pretty light yellow.

The two ships of the king were in a sort of open road, anchored to a spit of land with a bottom of coral where the cables were liable to be cut. The holding is good, in spite of the fact that the sea is often heavy and rough there. The island of New Cythera is presumed to be more extensive than the kingdom of France, although the crews of the two ships were able to explore only about one hundred leagues of the interior. The houses of these islanders are oblong, 35 or 40 feet long, and 15 or 16 feet wide; they are made of large reeds. The roofs of these cabins slope inwards; they are made of mats of reeds so tightly joined and so perfectly tied that neither rain nor the sun's heat can penetrate them. The air on this island is very pure and very healthy: the men afflicted with scurvy were cured there in five days. There are many simples, plants, and trees which promote good health; among these there is cardamine, a great antidote to scurvy. The physician-naturalist aboard the frigate has brought back a complete collection of these medicinal plants as well as collections of birds, dried fish, shells, and other curious rarities; some naturalists have even come down from Paris to Rochefort to see them.

The islanders are ignorant about medicine and about the use of drugs and remedies; they bleed themselves

26

when they are sick by scarification of the same veins as we do, making ligatures with strips of bark; they prick themselves with a piece of pointed mother-of-pearl, which serves as a lancet. They know about medicinal plants and use them against sickness, especially against the venereal diseases, which are common there and which are the same as those here in France.

The New Cytherians speak an unknown language which is quite limited; it cannot be compared to any other language or jargon. Their word for woman is *ainé* or *oyné*, for chicken they say *moé*, for bread they say *memi*, and for pig *ouan-rouen*. The islanders live in peace among themselves, and know neither hatred, quarrels, dissension, nor civil war; they have no offensive or defensive weapons. They only use bows and arrows, called *sasage*, which they carry on their shoulders and which they shoot with great dexterity in their contests; but these arrows are not armed with iron. The reed arrows which they use to hunt birds with are also without iron tips, and thus, when hit, the birds merely fall stunned to the ground; and so these arrows are not dangerous against men. On this island there are no lions, leopards, or tigers, nor are there any other savage beasts, snakes, or poisonous animals. These people are by nature vivacious and gay; their only musical instrument is a sort of flute, made of a reed called bamboo, which they play with their noses, and which makes quite an agreeable sound. They dance naturally and without any set order.

At first they considered the officers and crew to be gods: they paid them special homage; and when the astronomer-pilot used his globes and instruments to take a fix on the sun, or to make some astronomical observations, they were ready to worship him, thinking him a divinity. These islanders have neither temple, nor altar, nor a specially designated sacrificer: the first man there is simply chosen to kill the victim. The officers of the frigate saw two idols in the king's cabin: these statues of wood, which were quite natural, and crudely carved, are not really the object of any cult. The New Cytherians do not know anything of the major crimes: they abhor them, as do all well-policed and wise nations.

There are no titles of property among these islanders: all the wealth and everything produced on this island are communal.[8] The two ships left in New Cythera axes and other kinds of utensils, nails, locks, and pieces of iron of all kinds. After the islanders had seen what use a nail could be put to, they would give a pig in exchange for a single one; they would offer chickens and fruits in profusion for the smallest scraps of iron which they found so useful in holding their canoes together.

The New Cytherians know nothing of the duration or of the origin of their existence, and, caring little about the past, concern themselves only with the present. Their astonishment made it clear that they had never seen on their shores any other ships or any other men before the arrival of the two frigates:[9] they never tired of admiring the massiveness of these ships. The sound of the cannon particularly terrified them; and since they are extremely afraid of thunder, which is for them a sign of the anger of their divinity, they begged the officers not to shoot it off in the morning and evening. Our rifles, our pistols, and our side arms were also objects of horror to them. They haven't any knowledge whatsoever of writing or of the letters. Mr. de Bousagne, ensign on the *Boudeuse*, who has a great facility with languages, noticed that one of these islanders could pronounce the letters of our alphabet with great ease.

It is still uncertain if there are gold mines on the island, but it is known that a sailor who went ashore with some nails to do some trading was offered in exchange a piece of yellow metal which was thought to be gold.

The dead are exposed on a mat held up by four posts inside a covered and closed cabin; a man or a woman sits up with the dead day and night, until corruption and the worms force them to bury the body with its clothes.

The Marquis de Bougainville has brought back with him a Cytherian, and he has taken him to the court. This islander, who is 35 or 40 years old, would be very much missed on his island; he was accompanied everywhere by many women and by a crowd of people expressing their sadness and their wishes for his return.

From New Cythera the frigates went on to Batavia and then they sailed through the Straits of Java. They stopped at the Island of Rodrigue, a Dutch possession,

29

and anchored at Mauritius, capital of Ile de France and Bourbon, from which they brought home Mr. Daumas, the governor. They were careened at Mauritius on June 1, 1767;[10] they left there on the twenty-fourth,[11] and put in at the Cape of Good Hope, where they stayed only briefly. They brought on some sheep weighing from 100 to 120 pounds, and whose tails alone weighed from 20 to 25 pounds. They put in at the Island of Ascension, where they caught 100 turtles and brought back 46 of the smallest, weighing 500 pounds.

The storeship *Etoile*, which put in at Rochefort 20 days after the frigate *La Boudeuse*, which had left Mauritius 20 days before her, was laid up April 20, 1769.[12] This voyage, therefore, lasted from October 1766, to April 20, 1769. It will be noticed that Mr. de Bougainville covered 22,500 leagues in his voyage, as he sailed a great deal in the East. Admiral Anson's voyage, which was also a circumnavigation of the world, covered only 8,000 leagues.

Facsimile

RELATION

De la découverte que vient de faire Mr. de BOUGUAINVILLE, d'une Isle qu'il a nommée LA NOUVELLE CYTHERE.

MR. de Bouguainville commandant la Fregate du Roi La Boudeuse, armée à Brest de 32 Canons & 230 hommes d'Équipage, sur laquelle le Prince d'Orange étoit embarqué comme Passager, est parti de cette Rade en Octobre 1766, ayant sous ses ordres la Flute du Roi l'Étoile de Rochefort, armée de 20 Canons & de 200 hommes, commandée par Mr. de Giraudays, Capitaine de Brulot.

On avoit embarqué sur ces deux Batimens, qui ont fait le tour du monde par le detroit de Magellan dans la mer du Sud, Mr. de Romainville, Ingenieur; Mr. Camereau, Médecin Naturaliste; & Mr. Veson son Pilote Astronome.

Ces deux Batimens sont partis ensemble de la Rade de Rio-Janeiro pour se rendre à Montevideo afin d'hiverner, & se mettre ensuite en état de passer le Détroit de Magellan, ce qui ne peut se faire que depuis le mois de Janvier jusques à la fin d'Avril.

Ce Détroit de Magellan est un goulet ou canal assez étroit, borné des deux côtés de terres & d'Isles la plûpart habitées. Il y a entr'autres dans ce Détroit une Isle où les hommes sont d'une taille gigantesque; les plus petits d'entr'eux ont de huit à huit pieds & demi de hauteur, sont blancs & vivent en sauvages.

Ces deux Batimens du Roi ont passé par le Détroit de Bosthoon, ont pris connoissance des Isles orientales Hollandoises où sont les mines de diamans & de pierres precieuses, ils ont reconnu Sumatra, & ont mouillé à l'Isle Saftadia, Colonie supérieure à l'Isle de France.

Entre le Détroit de Magellan & de Batavia, latitude **** (Il n'a pas été possible de la sçavoir, M. de Bouguainville ayant défendu avant son départ de rien communiquer à ce sujet) est une ISLE nouvellement découverte par ces deux Batimens du Roi, nommée unanimement par le Corps des Officiers LA NOUVELLE CYTHERE. Le climat y est doux & tempéré, l'air pur & serain, & sous un très-beau Ciel. Les habitans de cette Isle sont fort grands, les hommes ayant de six à six pieds & demi de hauteur, & les femmes à peu-près de même taille. Ces Insulaires sont blancs, leur sang est beau. Les femmes surtout y sont distinguées par la regularité de leurs traits, leur douceur & leur affabilité naturelle. Les deux sexes ont les dents très-belles, & les cheveux de differentes couleurs, comme les Européens. Les hommes se laissent croître la barbe, & sont vêtus d'une pouche ou espece de dalmatique d'écorce d'arbre blanche qu'ils filent & cardent eux mêmes. Ils n'ont point de chaussure ni de culotes, & vont tête nue. Les femmes sont couvertes depuis le col jusques aux pieds d'un grand voile d'écorce d'arbre blanche & très-fine. Elles sont très-accueillantes, fort gracieuses & même caressantes. Lorsqu'elles rencontroient quelqu'un des Officiers ou autres gens de l'Equipage des deux Batimens, elles alloient au-devant d'eux, leur exprimant leur joye par des chants & des gestes démonstratifs, leur pressoient ensuite les mains, & enveloient dans leur voile l'Européen qu'elles avoient si bien accueilli. Leurs maris regardoient comme un homage & un honneur les préferences de tendresse pour leurs femmes; elles ne connoissent point

A

le vil intérêt , & toute leur ambition se borne à une pendeloque , ou à un bouton de manche qu'elles s'attachent à leurs oreilles. Elles ont une tendresse extrême pour leurs enfans.

Ces Insulaires ont un Roi auquel ils obéissent aveuglement ; il a sur eux droit de vie & de mort. Ces peuples adorent le Soleil comme une premiere Divinité ; ils en admettent ensuite deux autres , l'une présidant au bien & l'autre au mal. Ils offrent & décernent au Dieu bienfaisant les prémices des fruits & productions de la terre , au Génie ou Dieu malfaisant ils immolent des victimes humaines ; les femmes ne sont point soumises à une loi si cruelle. Les ouragans, les tempêtes & autres calamités publiques , sont le triste signal de ces sacrifices barbares , exécutés par l'ordre & la volonté du Roi. On choisit parmi eux le plus laid, celui qui a quelque membre contrefait , ou qui n'est pas aussi blanc que les autres , & on le dévoue en victime au Dieu malfaisant : on le couronne de fleurs , & un grand concours de peuple l'accompagne jusqu'au rivage , où on l'égorge cruellement en le saignant à la jugulaire avec une espece de couteau de nacre , ou pierre tranchante. On expose la victime immolée sur une claye ; on lui met tous les ornemens qui lui ont servi pendant sa vie ; on les rougit du sang de la victime , & nul Insulaire n'oseroit y toucher , ni se les approprier , crainte d'être exposé lui seul au courroux & à la vengeance du Dieu mal-faisant.

Ces Peuples n'ont fait jusques à présent ni commerce ni trafic ; ils ont de petites piroques assez mal construites & mal jointes , n'ayant point connu jusques à cette découverte l'usage des clous, de l'étoupe & du brayt : ils se servent de ces piroques pour faire leur pêche ; ils ont outre leur Roi, douze Chefs. Ce Roi n'a aucune marque de distinction, si ce n'est que sa cabane est un peu plus spacieuse ; & sa Souveraineté est héreditaire. Le sol de ce vaste Pays produit naturellement des cannes de sucre : mais ce Peuple n'en connoît ni l'usage ni la propriété. Le terrein est propre à toutes les plantations & productions de nos Isles de l'Amerique méridionale. Le fruit qui leur sert de pain , est de la grosseur d'un melon , pésant depuis deux jusques à dix livres ; il est rouge en dedans , & d'un très-bon goût : on le paîtrit avec de l'eau : on en fait une pâte , qui est une nourriture aussi substantielle que le pain , & qui peut se conserver fraîche cinq à six mois. Il y a aussi dans cette Isle des figues bananes , beaucoup meilleures que celles de St. Domingue & de la Martinique : il y en a qui sont de la grosseur de la cuisse. Ces Insulaires ont pour nourriture le Cochon, la Chevre & la Poule , à peu près semblables à ceux de l'Europe ; ils mangent les viandes roties sur des charbons , ou bouillies ; ils n'ont d'autre breuvage que l'eau de coco , & l'eau de roche , qui est beaucoup plus legere que la nôtre , suivant l'analyse qu'en a fait le Médecin naturaliste.

Ils mangent & boivent quand ils y sont invités par la faim & par la soif, sans avoir d'heures marquées pour leur repas ; ils mangent assis sur des nattes de jonc , & boivent dans des vases de coco. Leurs alimens sont, comme il a déja été dit , des viandes grillées ou bouillies , des poissons qu'ils prenent avec des hameçons de nacre , & dans des paniers ou filets à peu près semblables à ceux de nos Pêcheurs : les mets leur sont servis dans des vases de coco.

Il y a dans cette Isle beaucoup d'oiseaux très-rares, très-beaux & très-curieux , entr'autres le *Lorry*, dont le plumage est varié des plus belles & éclatantes couleurs. Il y a des Perruches ou Perriches de toute espece & de toutes couleurs : une espece entr'autres de la grosseur d'un Roitelet, dont le plumage est du plus beau bleu de Roi, & dont la queue est très-longue. Le Catacon, autrement dit *Pitacus-albus*, est un Perroquet blanc com-

me un Cigne , portant un gros bec noir , & au renversement , ainsi qu'au-
dessous du col , une hupe ou espece de crete renversée, d'un beau jeaune
clair. Les deux Bâtimens du Roi étoient mouillés dans une espece de rade
foraine a une enclavure de terre sur un fonds de roche de corail , où les
cables sont exposés à s'érailler. Sa tenue y est bonne , quoique les mers
y soient souvent très-grosses & bien agitées. L'Isle de la Nouvelle Cythére
a plus d'étendue , à ce que l'on présume , que le Royaume de France , quoique les équipages de ces Frégates n'ayent pû pénétrer & parcourir qu'environ cent lieues des côtes interieures. Les cases ou habitations de ces Insulaires sont de forme oblonque d'environ 35 ou 40 pieds de long , sur
15 ou 16 de large , & formées avec de gros roseaux. La couverture de
ces cabanes est faite en talus au-dedans , & formée avec des nattes de jonc
si étroitement jointes & si parfaitement liées , qu'elles sont impénétrables à
la pluye & à l'ardeur du Soleil. L'air qu'on respire dans cette Isle , est
très-pur & très-salutaire ; les scorbutiques des Frégates y ont été guéris en
5 jours. Il y a quantité de simples , de plantes & d'arbres très-favorables à
la santé , entr'autres la cressonette , souverain antidote contre le scorbut. Le
Médecin naturaliste embarqué sur la Frégate , en a raporté une collection
complete , ainsi que d'oiseaux , de poissons déssechés , de coquillage , de ra-
retés curieuses : il est même venu des Naturalistes pour les voir , de Paris
à Rochefort.

Ces Insulaires ignorent la médecine & l'usage des drogues & des remèdes ;
ils se seignent dans leurs maladies par scarification , sur les mêmes vaines
que nous , apres s'être fait une ligature avec une bande d'écorce d'arbre ;
ils se piquent avec un morceau de nacre pointu , qui leur tient lieu de lan-
cette. Ils connoissent l'usage des simples , & s'en servent dans leur maladie,
sur-tout dans les maladies véneriennes qui y sont communes , de même nature qu'en Europe. Les nouveaux Cythériens ont un langage inconnu, assez
bref : on ne peut se comparer à aucune langue ni jargon. Pour dire une
femme, *Ainé* ou *Oyné* , une poule, *Moé* , du pain, *Memi* , un cochon, *Ouan-
rouen.* Les Insulaires vivent en paix parmi eux, ne connoissent ni les hai-
nes, ni les querelles, ni les dissentions, ni les guerres intestines ; ils ignorent l'usage des armes offensives & défensives ; ils se servent seulement d'arcs
& de fleches , qu'on appelle *safage* , qu'ils balancent sur l'épaule , & qu'ils
jettent avec beaucoup de dexterité dans leur exercice de lutte ou de joutte ;
mais ces fleches n'étant point armées de fer, non plus que celles de roseau
dont ils se servent pour abbattre les oiseaux, qui tombent seulement etour-
dis , ne sont ni assez meurtrieres pour les tuer, ni assez dangereuses pour
nuire aux hommes. Il n'y a dans cette Isle ni Lion , ni Léopard , ni Tigre ,
ni bête sauvage , non plus que des Serpens & autres bêtes vénimeuses. Ces
Peuples sont naturellement d'humeur vive & joyeuse ; ils ne connoissent pour
tout instrument de musique , qu'une espece de flûte , taillée avec un roseau,
appellée *Banbou* , dont ils jouent avec le nez , & dont ils tirent des sons
assez harmonieux. Ils dansent naturellement & sans ordre. Ils ont d'abord
regardé les Officiers & les gens de l'Equipage comme des Dieux : ils leur
rendoient des hommages particuliers ; & lorsque le Pilote Astronome s'est
servi de ses globes & de ses instrumens pour prendre la hauteur & obser-
ver le Soleil , ou pour faire ses observations astronomiques , ils étoient prêts
à l'adorer, le regardant comme une Divinité. Ces Insulaires n'ont ni Temple, ni Autel , ni Sacrificateur désigné : le premier venu d'entr'eux est nom-
mé pour égorger la victime. Les Officiers des Frégates virent chez le Roi

4

deux idoles, ou Statues de bois affez naturelles, & groffierement taillées : ces deux Statues n'ont point d'objet de culte reel. Les nouveaux Cythe-riens ne connoiffent point les grands crimes ; ils les ont même en hor-reur, comme toutes les Nations fages & policées.

Il n'y a point de fure de propriété parmi ces Infulaires ; tous les biens & toutes les productions de l'Ifle font en commun. Les deux Fregates ont laiffé dans la nouvelle Cythére des haches & autres fortes d'uftenfiles, des clous, ferrures & ferramentes de toute efpece. Quand ces Infulaires ont vû l'ufage que l'on faifoit des clous, ils donnoient un cochon pour un feul clou ; ils don-noient des poules & des fruits a profufion pour les moindres ferremens, dont ils trouvoient l'ufage commode pour confolider leurs pirroques.

Ces nouveaux Cytheriens ne connoiffent point d'Ere ni d'origine à leur exif-tence, & peu foucieux du paffé, le préfent feul les affecte. Ils ont donné a entendre par leur etonnement qu'ils n'avoient jamais vû fur leurs Côtes d'au-tres Vaiffeaux ni d'autres hommes que ceux des deux Fregates. Ils ne pou-voient fe laffer d'admirer ces maffes énormes. Le bruit du canon fur-tout les epouvanta ; & comme ils craignent extrememet le tonnerre, étant une preu-ve pour eux du courroux de leur Divinité, ils prierent les Officiers de ne point le faire tirer le matin ni le foir. Nos fufils, nos piftolets & nos armes blanches etoient encor des objets d'horreur pour eux : Ils n'ont pas même la moindre connoiffance de l'écriture ni des caractères Mr. de Boufagne, Enfeigne de Vaiffeau fur la Boudeufe, ayant beaucoup de facilité pour l'idiome des langues, a remarque de la part de quelqu'un de ces Infulaires beaucoup de fa-cilité à prononcer les lettres de notre Alphabet.

On eft encore incertain s'il y a des mines d'or dans cette Ifle ; on a feulement connoiffance qu'un matelot des Fregates ayant porté à terre des clous pour les trafiquer, un de ces Infulaires lui donna en échange un morceau de métal jaune qu on croit être de l'or.

On expofe les morts fur une claye élevée & foutenue de quatre piliers, dans une cabane clofe & couverte ; un homme ou une femme y veille jour & nuit, jufques à ce que la corruption & les vers les forcent à les inhumer avec leurs vetemens.

M. le Marquis de Bougainville a amené un Cythérien, & l'a conduit à la Cour. Cet Infulaire âgé de 35 à 40 ans parut être fort regreté dans l'Ifle ; il etoit accompagné par-tout de beaucoup de femmes, d'un grand concours de peuple, exprimant leur regret, & faifant des vœux pour fon retour.

De la Nouvelle Cythére, les Fregates ont été à Batavia, d'ou elles font par-fies pour doubler le Detroit de Java. Dans la poffeffion Hollandoife elles ont re-connu l'Ifle de Rodrigue, & ont mouillé à Maurice, Capitale des Ifles de Fran-ce & de Bourbon, d'où elles ont ramené Mr. Daumas, Gouverneur. Elles ont caréné à Maurice le 1. Juin 1767 ; elles font parties le 24, & ont relaché au Cap de Bonne-Efperance ou elles ont fait très-peu de féjour. Elles ont apporté des moutons pefans de 100 à 120 livres. dont la feule queue pefe de 20 à 25 L. Elles ont relaché à l'Ifle de l Afcenfion on elles ont chaviré cent Tortues, & en ont raporté 46 des plus petites, pefant 500 Livres.

Le défarmement de la Flute l'Etoile, qui eft arrivée à Rochefort 20 jours plus tard que la Fregate la Boudeufe . . . . qui etoit partie de Maurice 20 jours avant cette Flute, s'eft fait le 20 Avril 1769. Ce voyage a donc duré depuis le mois d'Octobre 1766, jufqu au 20 avril 1769. On remarque que Mr. de Bou-guainville a fait 22500 lieues dans fon voyage, ayant beaucoup navigué dans la partie de l'Eft. Le voyage de l'Amiral Anfon, qui eft auffi celui du tour du Monde, n'a été que de 8000 Lieues.

Commentary

EW CYTHERA, or Tahiti is the focal point of the *Newsletter*; the circumnavigation is apparently only of casual interest. This emphasis may be misplaced, but it is understandable, especially in a newsletter, for the story of the island is more exciting than another voyage.

No mention whatsoever is made of the Malouine Islands or their relation in political terms to Bougainville's mission. The fact that Bougainville first claimed these islands for a French colony and then had to turn them over to Spain is passed over in complete silence — to the reader of the *Newsletter* the voyage seems to have begun in Rio de Janeiro and to have had no specific purpose at all. There is also a failure to mention the search for the austral continent which was such an important part of the reason for the expedition. The omission of the Malouine Islands at the start and the austral quest at the end of the account isolates Bougainville's discovery of

Tahiti and blurs the general picture of his expedition almost beyond recognition.

To restore to Bougainville's voyage something of its original dimension and thereby correct and complement the *Newsletter*'s report of it, one must turn to the full version given in his own *Voyage autour du Monde* and review the sequence of events as recounted there.

Bougainville set sail from Nantes on Saturday, November 15, 1766, on the frigate *Boudeuse*, but soon ran into such stormy weather that he was forced to put in at Brest for repairs: the ship was quite extensively overhauled, and finally weighed anchor on December 5. The storeship, *Etoile*, under the command of La Giraudais, set out from Rochefort on February 1, 1767. The two ships were supposed to meet eventually at the Malouine Islands.

Bougainville landed at Montevideo without further incident on February 1, went briefly to Buenos Aires to arrange with the Spanish for the transfer of the colony, and then, accompanied by three Spanish ships, headed for the Malouine Islands. Once the ceremonies of transferal were accomplished, Bougainville anxiously awaited the arrival of the *Etoile*; when it failed to come, he set out for Rio de Janeiro, the alternate meeting place. Here at last he joined up with the *Etoile*, and the two ships then returned to Montevideo, where they took on provisions and made necessary repairs in preparation for the next part of the voyage.

At this point in *Voyage autour du Monde*, Bougain-ville inserted a very lively account of the Jesuit missions in the Spanish territories near Montevideo, with stories of abuse and scandal and of the dramatic events that put an end to an empire within an empire. He concluded this lengthy digression on the expulsion of the Jesuits from South America — a most important historic event — by commenting that being present during the revolution in these missions was one of the most interesting experiences of his voyage — a somewhat laconic conclusion in view of the great historic importance of this event.

This historic interlude, however, represents a delay in fulfilling the goals of the voyage, and when at last all repairs were completed, Bougainville set sail from Mon-tevideo on November 14, 1767, with a sense of being be-hind schedule: already a year had elapsed and he was just preparing to make his way to the Straits of Magel-lan. The account of the long passage of the Straits in *Voyage autour du Monde* is replete with incidents. In particular, it contains a description of the Patagonians and the affirmation that these people are not giants, de-spite what certain Englishmen may have said. It also presents a bleak picture of the Pécherais, a pathetic and miserable people living at the tip of the continent whose plight would disabuse even the most determined dreamer of his belief that the primitive life is naturally the Edenic one.

During the voyage through the Straits, accurate accounts of the movements of his ships were kept, with records of all the particulars of the various harbors or possible anchorages on charts which would be of real service to those sailors who followed his route in the future. Bougainville reported that the statements made by other navigators concerning the direction of tides in the Straits were untrue; and, in one of the few outbursts which he permitted himself, he condemned those who excised from their accounts of voyages all the navigational science that was in reality their substance:

How many times we regretted not having the journals of Narborough and Beauchesne in their original state, and having instead to consult disfigured and incomplete versions: not only do the compilers of these selections have a mania for cutting out whatever pertains only to navigation, but also they don't know a word of the sailor's language, so that if by chance some detail connected with navigation remains, they replace it with nonsense. Their only purpose is to make a work agreeable to the effeminate of both sexes, and the only result is the concoction of a book which bores everyone and is useful to nobody.[1]

The vehemence of Bougainville's stricture is understandable on the part of a sailor who spent fifty-two days in a difficult pass. But Bougainville himself, when preparing the account of his voyage, wrote for the interested general reader and omitted much navigational information. In evaluating Bougainville's work in geography, however, it should be noted that he was the first navigator before Cook to take systematic longitude readings at sea —

a practice which led to more accurate knowledge about the width of the Pacific.

After the Straits the weather was favorable, and the two ships then headed into the Pacific. From the end of January until the beginning of April Bougainville and his men sailed west, increasingly anxious to discover a harbor with fresh water and supplies. They had come upon many an isolated but inhabited island (how did man happen to be here, Bougainville wondered), had named some, and had taken possession of others in the name of France. These islands had not been accessible for their ships, however; rations were by now growing direly short and sickness was increasing, so that when in the first days of April they sighted a large island and saw that it offered anchorage, they were understandably relieved. As the ships approached, the natives of the island crowded about in their little craft and what ensued is best described by Bougainville himself:

The crowd of dugouts was so thick around the ships that we had a great deal of trouble anchoring. All the inhabitants came toward us crying *tayo*, which means friend, and making gestures of friendship: they asked for nails and earrings. The dugouts were filled with women whose faces were as beautiful as most European women's, and whose bodies were more beautiful. Most of these nymphs were naked, since the men and old women who accompanied them had taken off the nymphs' robes. These women at first made signs to us from the dugouts, and in spite of their naïveté, one could make out in their gestures a slight embarrassment, either because nature has embellished women everywhere with a certain timidity, or because, even in coun-

43

tries where the openness of the Golden Age still exists, women pretend not to want what they in fact most desire. The men, more simple or more free, expressed themselves more clearly: they urged us to choose a woman and to follow her to land, and their unequivocal gestures made it plain how we were to treat her. I ask you, how was one to keep four hundred young French sailors, who hadn't seen women in six months, at their work in the midst of such a spectacle? Despite all the precautions which we took, a young girl got on board and came onto the forecastle and stood by one of the hatchways which are over the capstan. The girl negligently let fall her robe and stood for all to see, as Venus stood forth before the Phrygian shepherd; and she had the celestial shape of Venus. The sailors and soldiers rushed to get at the hatchway, and never was a capstan turned with such eagerness.

We managed to restrain these bedeviled men, however, but it was no less difficult to control oneself.[2]

It is fitting that the joy of discovering a much-needed refuge, combined with the elation that such a happy prospect as the reception on the island conjured up, should have prompted Bougainville to name this place New Cythera. The real name of the island was, of course, Tahiti, but his choice of a new name reflected the notion of an earthly paradise which persisted in his imagination. Bougainville noted in his journal, for instance, that

Nature had placed the island in the most perfect climate in the world, had embellished it with every pleasing prospect, had endowed it with all its riches, and filled it with large, strong, and beautiful people. Nature herself dictated the laws. The inhabitants follow them in peace and constitute perhaps the happiest society which the world knows. Lawmakers and philosophers, come here and look upon the establishment of what your im-

44

agination could not even conceive. Moreover, one hopes for the sake of these people that Nature has refused to produce here the objects of Europe's cupidity; they need only the fruits which the land provides in abundance, and the rest, by drawing us Europeans here, would only bring to them the evils of the iron age. Farewell, happy and wise people; remain always as you are now. I will always remember you with delight, and as long as I live I will celebrate the happy island of Cythera: it is the true Utopia.[3]

And so Bougainville sensed that the arrival of his ships might somehow signify the destruction of this innocent land. He expressed this sorrowful (and prophetic) intuition in his picture of the meeting of the Europeans and the Tahitians. The scene seems almost symbolic:

The islanders hardly knew how to express their joy at receiving us. The head of this canton took us to his house and led us in. Inside, there were five or six women and a venerable old man. The women greeted us by putting their hands on their chests and saying *tayo* several times. The old man was the father of our host; he had all the marks of respectability conferred by great age and none of the traces of its decrepitude. This venerable man hardly seemed to notice our arrival; he even withdrew without answering our gestures of friendship, showing neither fear, astonishment, nor curiosity. Far from sharing the ecstasy which the sight of us caused in all these people, he seemed careworn and deep in thought, as if he feared that these days of happiness consecrated to repose would be troubled by the arrival of a new race.[4]

And yet the *Newsletter* is remarkably objective in its account of Tahiti. It presents an accurate if often unflattering vision of the island and its people. Indeed, the striking feature of the report is precisely the unsentimental portrayal of defects and vices which the very name of New Cythera tended to obscure: the island paradise is replete with human sacrifices, warfare, and slavery, and its social order is hierarchical, its political organization tyrannical. The alluring picture often drawn of primitive society in the eighteenth century is here countered by a realistic one in which none of the brutishness is passed over in silence. Bougainville knew all these things about the Tahitians, and yet he could not help but cherish the fond illusion — for him Tahiti was like a friend whom one loves despite all imperfections.

After a stay of just ten days, Bougainville set out on the long search for the austral lands; the goal of his navigation now was to locate what he knew as the Terre-du-Saint-Esprit, the land of the Holy Spirit. In the *Histoire des Navigations aux Terres Australes* of Charles de Brosses, which Bougainville had studied with great interest, a report made by Ferdinand de Queiros to the king of Spain was quoted: ". . . The size of the lands we have recently discovered equals the size of all of Europe and of Asia Minor as far as the Caspian Sea. . . . The land which we have been over the most thoroughly, below the fifteenth parallel, is preferable to Europe . . ."[5] Bougainville's secret instructions from the king of France explicitly stated that "he was to search out those lands lying between the west coast of America and the Indies

46

which various navigators had seen, and which were
named Terres de Diemen, Nouvelle-Hollande, Carpen-
tarie, *Terre-du-Saint-Esprit*, Nouvelle-Guinée, etc. Since
these islands, or continent, are only imperfectly known,
it would be interesting to learn more about them; and
since no European nation has colonies or rights on these
lands, it would be a great advantage for France to recog-
nize them and take possession of them, if they could advance her commerce and navigation. With this in mind,
Bougainville should pay special attention to the area
from 40 degrees south latitude toward the north . . ."[6]
This Bougainville did, but with an increasing sense that
his mission would prove fruitless. Meanwhile, supplies
were running dangerously low, the morale of the ships'
company had deteriorated, and the perilous navigation
filled the captain with dread that his expedition would
end in shipwreck in the unknown and reef-filled sea. At
last Bougainville decided to turn back and sail north,
and then to head for some charted ports. The official
writer of the *Boudeuse*, St. Germain, expressed the general sense of relief brought by this change of course, and
at the same time affirmed that this turning back was in a
sense an admission of defeat, for, as he wrote, "the land
which we were looking for was the Terre-du-Saint-Esprit
(the purpose of our mission was none other than this),
from which we would get nutmeg and cinnamon . . ."[7]

The next long part of the voyage was dominated by
the need to find relief from the ravages of sickness and

the threat of starvation. The memory of Tahiti served to highlight the present miseries, for all the islands they now came upon seemed to be either barren or inhabited by warlike peoples. Increasingly, Bougainville's account reports carnage (which he deplored), and the heavenly vision of the primitive society incarnated in New Cythera is replaced by scenes of unregenerate savagery.

All during this time, however, Bougainville was making useful geographic discoveries, thus contributing his part in the great Anglo-French "collaboration" to chart this region. The vast continent imagined earlier was being gradually atomized: innumerable islands and indeed a small continent, Australia, replaced it on the map. Captain Cook would boast in 1772 after his first voyage that he had made great passages and bays in the imaginary austral land mass, and Bougainville could lay a similar, if less grandiose, claim to having "created" straits where before it was thought there were none. This famine-haunted segment of his circumnavigation became in fact a search for a passage from the Pacific into the Sea of the Moluccas, and Bougainville's achievement was commemorated by two passages named for him, one in the New Hebrides and the other in the Solomon Islands.

But at this juncture, by Bougainville's own estimate, if there had been another eight days at sea many of his crew would have died and the rest would have all become gravely ill. Happily, the ships at last came to the island of Boeroe, a Dutch port, in which the starving

Frenchmen found hospitality as well as good and abundant food. The sense of relief which had cast a glow over Bougainville's landing at Tahiti now operated to transform this small colonial outpost in the Moluccas into a sort of European paradise, which conjured up if not the pleasures of home, then at least its comforts. An approximation of the former would soon, as it turned out, be provided by the reception given the French at Batavia.

Bougainville paid close attention to the Dutch organization of the spice trade, and his account of that nation's colonial empire parallels the picture he had drawn earlier of the Jesuit "empire" in South America. Like the Jesuits' closed policies, Holland's protective policy of destroying spice plants on all but well-controlled possessions and of maintaining secrecy about navigation in these seas did not succeed in keeping jealous powers out. In each case, Bougainville witnessed the breaking up of a monopoly. Everywhere he felt the encroaching presence of the English; moreover, his patent interest in these affairs suggests that France was also most anxious to take a share in the prize that Holland had once held so firmly and so exclusively.

On November 8, 1768, Bougainville arrived at the Ile de France, which was the next scheduled port of call, the next to last before the return to France. The stay in this French colony whetted the appetite for France herself, and, once his ships had been repaired and stores laid aboard, Bougainville was anxious to head for his native land. On December 12, 1768, after a month's sojourn and an informative inspection of the colony, he set out in the *Boudeuse*, leaving the *Etoile* to follow later. The next port was at the Cape of Good Hope, where Bougainville again admired the Dutch colonial organization. It was in the middle of January when the ship left the tip of Africa; on February 5, it was anchored at Ascension. Bougainville and his crew, delighted with a remarkably large catch of turtles from the previous day's fishing in this harbor, set sail early in the morning of February 6 with the knowledge that when they next dropped anchor they would be home. On March 16, 1769, two years and four months after she had left Nantes, the *Boudeuse* entered the port of Saint-Malo. Nearly a month later, on April 24, the *Etoile* anchored in the port of Rochefort.

By March 19, Bougainville had arrived at Versailles, and on the twenty-first he was received by the Duc de Choiseul and César-Gabriel Praslin, the ministers who had favored Bougainville's undertaking and were now eager for a report on its success. Bougainville gave a detailed account of the lands he had discovered, or "recovered," and described the advantages that could be derived from them. Here was the possibility of a new empire whose riches might compensate France for the losses sustained in the Seven Years War. But he cautioned that haste would be required, for the English were already prowling: indeed Bougainville was aware that he had been preceded in much of his voyage by them. He had learned at Batavia of the expeditions of Wallis and Carteret, and had actually hailed Carteret on the *Swallow* as he passed it on the return leg of his voyage — this "race" to catch up with and overtake the Englishman, described by Bougainville at the end of *Voyage autour du Monde*, was symbolic of the rivalry France felt toward England, which was a prime motivation for the circumnavigation he had just completed.

After having informed the two ministers of the salient points of his expedition, Bougainville was granted an audience with King Louis XV.

Bougainville soon became a celebrity in Paris and at the court, not just because of his discovery of Tahiti but more specifically because of the New Cytherian, Aoutourou, whom he had brought back with him. Aoutourou, the son of a Tahitian prince, was formally presented to the king at the end of April 1769, but before and after this date he was scrutinized, studied, discussed, and admired by scientists, philosophers, and linguists: Bougainville's protégé was that most interesting of all eighteenth-century phenomena — a noble savage.

By the end of October 1769, Bougainville had drawn up his account of the entire expedition, his *Voyage autour du Monde*, and presented it to the king. The voyage had proved to be of considerable scientific interest and had increased national confidence in France's overseas empire and in her ability to compete in the race for possessions. On the other hand, Bougainville had failed to make a commercial success of his voyage. There had been hopes that he would be able to establish on Ile de France a lucrative spice trade and that his passage through the Moluccas would allow him to collect the precious spice plants that were a form of gold; but these hopes had come to nothing. It was an open secret that Bougainville wished to be named governor of the newly claimed regions and to establish French colonies about the island of New Cythera. Unfortunately, however, the royal treasury lacked the means to support colonial ventures. And the patronage and financial support from other sources that might have followed upon commercial success were also not forthcoming. Bougainville was, therefore, not to realize his ambition to return to the South Seas.

In one sense, the adventure had come to an end; in another, the impact of the voyage continued to be felt through the literary, scientific, moral, and philosophical reverberations it generated.

The philosophes and the sensationalists used the *Newsletter*, Bougainville's *Voyage autour du Monde*, and the reports of his companions for their own purposes. While the sensationalists seized on the fantastic and mythological elements which Bougainville himself had refuted, the philosophes used the material on Tahiti to illustrate certain of their theories about man's natural state.

The account of Tahitian mores in Bougainville's report seems to have stimulated the moral and philosophical speculations of the French philosopher Diderot in his famous *Supplément au Voyage de Bougainville (ou Dialogue entre A. et B. sur L'inconvénient d'attacher des idées morales à certaines actions physiques qui n'en comportent pas)*; but it was probably Philibert Commerson's interpretation, rather than Bougainville's, that had the greater influence on Diderot. Commerson, the naturalist who accompanied Bougainville, published his account of the expedition in 1769; it was distinctly reshaped by what the French *philosophe* Diderot would refer to as the "fable d'Otaiti."[8] Commerson began by naming Tahiti Utopia, referring to Thomas More's ideal republic, and elaborated according to his Rousseauean bias:

There neither shame nor modesty exercises its tyranny: the lightest veil floats away in the breeze and in accord with human desire: the act of procreation is a religious one. The prelude to it is encouraged by the wishes and the songs of all the people assembled, and its climax is celebrated by universal applause. Every foreigner is invited to participate in these happy mysteries; indeed, it is one of the duties of hospitality to invite strangers to attend to them, so that the good Utopian is constantly either enjoying his own pleasure or the spectacle of others'. Some censor with clerical bands may perhaps see in this only the breakdown of manners, horrible prostitution, and the most bald effrontery; but he will be profoundly mistaken in his conception of natural man, who is born essentially good, free of every prejudice, and who follows, without defiance and without remorse, the gentle impulses of instinct not yet corrupted by reason.[9]

Since Commerson was a widely respected member of France's scientific elite, his evocation of Tahiti was highly influential. Ironically, Bougainville became identified with this colorful version, instead of with his own more sober one.

Although the names of Bougainville and Diderot are linked together for all time by virtue of the *Supplément*, it would be a grave error to assume that Diderot was entirely approving of the Bougainville expedition. Diderot and the other contemporary philosophes were basically anticolonialists as well as pacifists. And at least one way to read Diderot's *Supplément* is as an anticolonial tract. The second section, which is called "Les Adieux du vieillard" is a clear and eloquent condemnation of colonialism, and thus a direct attack on men like Bougainville. The political objectives which Bougainville shared with such important governmental figures as the Duc de Choiseul are implicitly denounced as barbaric by Diderot's imagined character of the wise old man, who is also a noble savage. The Treaty of Paris of 1763 had caused the philosophes to revise their conception of colonialism and, particularly, to attack the companies which had officially protected monopolies and traded in slaves. They challenged the colonial pact and, by the end of the century, came to question the legitimacy of colonization itself; finally they stated that decolonization should be initiated.

Bougainville was very far from holding these ideas. He had a more realistic notion of commerce and knew that if there was to be trade there must be colonies set up to create markets and exchange. This was precisely one of Bougainville's objectives on his trip — to take possession of any newly discovered lands which might prove beneficial to the trade of his country.

Another noted philosophe, Voltaire, wrote about Bougainville and Tahiti in his *Les Oreilles du Comte de Chesterfield et le Chapelain Goudman*, published in 1775. While Voltaire was concerned about the impact Europeans might have on the Tahitian way of life, he believed that trade would be useful in establishing an international community whose self-interest would put it above the struggles of national ambition and thus act as a deterrent to war — something he found extremely distasteful. The loss of Canada by France to England, which seemed such a catastrophe to Bougainville, is briefly and bitterly commented upon by Voltaire in a famous passage in *Candide*: "You know that these two nations are fighting over a few acres of snow somewhere near Canada and that they are spending much more money on this beautiful war than all of Canada is worth."[10]

Bougainville's voyage has suffered many "deformations" (not the least of which is the editing and cutting that his account has been subjected to — there is no complete or reliable edition of *Voyage autour du Monde* currently available), and yet it seems incontrovertible that the influence of his circumnavigation has also been extended by the fascinating moral and philosophic speculations which it generated.

Notes

PAGES 3–18

1. Basil Williams, *The Life of William Pitt* (2 vols., London, 1913), Vol. II, p. 330.
2. Maurice Thiéry. *Bougainville: Soldier and Sailor* (London, 1932), p. 83.
3. Richard Walter, comp., *A Voyage round the World in the Years MDCCXL, I, II, III, IV by George Anson, Esq.* (London, 1748), pp. 90–92.
4. Jean-Etienne Martin-Allanic, *Bougainville: Navigateur et les Découvertes de son Temps* (2 vols., Paris, 1964), Vol. I, p. 100.

PAGES 21–30

1. The *Boudeuse* was actually commissioned in Nantes; but put in at Brest for repairs and sailed on December 5, some 20 days after his original start.
2. "Captain of a fire ship" is the term for officer in charge of any merchant ships on a long expedition.
3. The naturalist's name was Philibert Commerson. The pilot's name was Verron, or Véron.
4. Bougainville actually says between September and the end of March in *Voyage autour du Monde*.
5. This erroneous reporting concerns the fabled Patagonians. What Bougainville really noted was the following: "These men are of a good size; among the ones we saw, none was shorter than five feet five or six inches, and none taller than five feet nine or ten. The men of the *Etoile* had seen several men six feet tall during the previous trip. What seemed gigantic about them was the breadth of their shoulders, the size of their heads, and the thickness of their limbs. They are well fed, strong, and fit; they exemplify what man

left to nature and provided with good food grows to be . . ." *Voyage autour du Monde*, 2nd ed. (3 vols., Paris, 1772–73), Vol. I, pp. 242–243.

6. Bougainville was under orders to report to the king the findings of his voyage, which as noted above was both a political and a military enterprise, as well as a scientific one; this explains the secrecy. The position of the island of Tahiti was not disclosed in the first edition of Bougainville's *Voyage autour du Monde* either, but in the second edition it is given: "The island which we first called New Cythera is called Tahiti by its inhabitants. Its latitude of 17ᵈ 35′ 3″ at our camp was determined by several meridian altitudes of the sun taken with a quadrant on shore. Its longitude of 150ᵈ 40′ 17″ west of Paris has been fixed by eleven observations of the moon, according to the method of horary angles." *Ibid.*, Vol. II, p. 65.

7. Bougainville asserts that, on the contrary, they eat meat only very rarely: "vegetables and fish are their principal food. They rarely eat meat; children and young girls never eat it, and this undoubtedly helps keep them exempt from almost all our diseases." *Ibid.*, Vol. II, p. 75.

8. This is flatly contradicted by Bougainville. He had indeed, at first, thought all Tahitians equal, but soon had occasion to correct this impression: "I have said before that the inhabitants of Tahiti seemed to us to live in a happy state we might all envy. We thought them nearly equal among themselves, or at least benefiting from a freedom limited only by laws established to ensure the happiness of all. I was mistaken: the differences between ranks are very great in Tahiti, and clearly marked. Kings and important men have the power of life and death over their slaves and servants; I am even inclined to think that they have this barbarous power over common people whom they call *Tata-einou*, vile men — in any case, it is from this unfortunate class that victims for human sacrifice are chosen. Meat and fish are reserved for the tables of the great, the people live on vegetables and fruit. Even the manner of lighting differs according to class, and the kind of wood used by people of distinction is different from the kind the people are permitted to use. Only kings may plant *Weeping-willow* or *Tree of the great Lord* in front of their houses. By bending the branches of this tree and planting them in the ground it is possible to give to one's shade the direction and dimension one wants: in Tahiti this shade is the dining room of kings . . ." *Ibid.*, Vol. II, pp. 108–109.

9. Once again the information is not correct: "I learned from Aoutourou [the Tahitian whom Bougainville brought back to France with him] that an English ship had put in at his island about eight months before our arrival there. It was under the command of Mr. Wallis." *Ibid.*, Vol. II, p. 114.

10. According to Bougainville's account (see *Voyage*, Vol. II, pp. 389–390), this operation took place between November 16 and 18, 1768.

11. The *Boudeuse* set sail on December 12; the *Etoile* followed later. *Ibid.*, Vol. II, p. 393.

12. Bougainville put in at Saint-Malo on March 16, 1769. The *Etoile* arrived in France almost exactly one month later, anchoring in Rochefort on April 14. *Ibid.*, Vol. II, p. 412.

1. Louis Antoine de Bougainville, *Voyage autour du Monde* (Paris, 1771), p. 173.

2. *Ibid.*, pp. 189–191.

3. Bougainville's *Journal*, quoted in Jean-Etienne Martin-Allanic, *Bougainville: Navigateur et les Découvertes de son Temps* (2 vols., Paris, 1964), Vol. I, pp. 683–685.

4. Louis Antoine de Bougainville, *Voyage*, pp. 192–193.

5. Charles de Brosses, *Histoire des Navigations aux Terres Australes* (2 vols., Paris, 1756), Vol. II, p. 334.

6. Martin-Allanic, *Bougainville*, Vol. I, p. 714.

7. *Ibid.*, p. 724.

8. Denis Diderot, *Oeuvres Philosophiques* (5 vols., Brussels, 1829), Vol. III, pp. 58–59.

9. *Mercure de France* (Paris), November 1769, pp. 198–199.

10. François Marie Arouet de Voltaire, *Candide, ou l'Optimisme*, with Introduction by André Morize (Paris, 1931), pp. 171–172.

Bibliography

Relation de la Découverte que vient de faire Mr. de Bouguainville [sic], *d'une Isle quil a nommée La Nouvelle Cythere.* [n.p., 1769]. The translation in this volume is based on the copy in the James Ford Bell Library.

[News sheet in French on Bougainville's voyage around the world, issued in Paris, July 20, 1769.]

[News sheet in French on Bougainville's voyage around the world, issued in Marseilles, August 1, 1769.]

Louis Antoine de Bougainville. *Relazione della Scoperta fatta dal Sig. de Bouguainville* [sic] *d'un Isola ch'egli ha nominata la Nuova Cyterea.* Rome, Puccinelli, 1769.

Louis Antoine de Bougainville. *Voyage autour du Monde, par la Frégate du Roi La Boudeuse, et la Flûte l'Etoile; en 1766, 1767, 1768 & 1769.* Paris, Saillant & Nyon, 1771.

Louis Antoine de Bougainville. *Voyage autour du Monde, par la Frégate du Roi La Boudeuse, et la Flûte l'Etoile; en 1766, 1767, 1768 & 1769. Seconde édition, augmentée.* 2 volumes. Paris, Saillant & Nyon, 1772.

In this augmented edition of his *Voyage*, Bougainville has added an important *Discours préliminaire*; he also makes corrections pointed out by his English translator, Forster; mention is here also made of the voyages of Captain Cook.

Louis Antoine de Bougainville. *A Voyage round the World. Performed by Order of His Most Christian Majesty, in the Years 1766, 1767, 1768, and 1769.* London, J. Nourse and T. Davies, 1772. The first English edition of Bougainville's *Voyage*, translated by Johann Reinhold Forster.

Louis Antoine de Bougainville. *Reis rondom de Weereldt, gedaen op bevel des Konings van Frankrijk, in de Jaren 1766 tot 1769, met het Fregat La Boudeuse en het Fluitschip l'Etoile.* Dordrecht, Abraham Blussé en Zoon, 1772.

Supplément au Voyage de M. de Bougainville, ou Journal d'un Voyage autour du Monde, fait par MM. Banks & Solander, Anglois, en 1768, 1769, 1770, 1771. Traduit de l'Anglois, par M. de Fréville. Paris, Saillant & Nyon, 1772. This is a translation of the *Journal of a Voyage round the World, in His Majesty's Ship Endeavour, in the Years 1768, 1769, 1770, and 1771,* London, 1771. The same book exists under the title *Journal d'un Voyage autour du Monde, en 1768, 1769, 1770, 1771; contenant les divers evénemens du Voyage etc., traduit de l'Anglois, par M. de Fréville,* Paris, 1772.

Louis Antoine de Bougainville. *Voyage autour du Monde, par la Frégate du Roi La Boudeuse, et la Flûte l'Etoile; en 1766, 1767, 1768 & 1769. Nouvelle edition augmentée.* 2 volumes. Neuchâtel, Imprimerie de la Société Typographique, 1773. The only augmentation is the addition of a vocabulary of maritime terms; this is actually a reprinting of the first edition of 1771.

Supplément au Voyage de M. de Bougainville, ou Journal d'un Voyage autour du Monde, fait par MM. Banks & Solander, Anglois, en 1768, 1769, 1770, 1771. Tr. de l'Anglois, par M. de Fréville. Neuchâtel, Imprimerie de la Societé Typographique, 1773.

Anne François Joachim Fréville, *Histoire des nouvelles Découvertes faites dans la Mer du Sud en 1767, 1768, 1769 & 1770.* 2 volumes. Paris, De Hansy, 1774.

[Nicolas Bricaire de la Dixmerie] *Le Sauvage de Taïti aux Français; avec un Envoi au Philosophe Ami des Sauvages.* London, Paris; Le Jay, Libraire, 1790.

Denis Diderot. *Supplément au Voyage de Bougainville. Dialogue sur l'inconvénient d'attacher des Idées morales à certaines actions physiques qui n'en comportent pas.* First published in Simon Jérome Bourlet de Vauxcelles, editor, *Opuscules philosophiques et littéraires,* Paris, 1796.

Denis Diderot. Review of Bougainville's *Voyage,* published for the first time in Diderot, *Oeuvres complètes,* edited by J. Assézat and M. Tourneux, Volume 2, pp. 199–206. Paris, Garnier frères, 1875.

THIS *book, in Linotype Bodoni Book on Mohawk Superfine Text, was designed by Jane McCarthy of the University of Minnesota Press. It was composed, printed, and bound at the North Central Publishing Company of St. Paul. Of the limited edition of 750 copies this is copy*

62